Original title:
In the Glow of the Tropics

Copyright © 2025 Creative Arts Management OÜ
All rights reserved.

Author: Micah Sterling
ISBN HARDBACK: 978-1-80581-551-8
ISBN PAPERBACK: 978-1-80581-078-0
ISBN EBOOK: 978-1-80581-551-8

Crescendo in the Boughs of Life

Monkeys swing with silly glee,
Eating mangoes, wild and free.
Parrots squawk with vibrant flair,
While palm trees dance without a care.

Lizards lounge in sunlit spots,
Debating on their favorite knots.
Crickets chirp a lively tune,
As fireflies twirl 'neath the moon.

Bamboo shakes from laughter's fright,
A raccoon donned in shades so bright.
Coconuts fall with a thud,
While the sea breezes stir up a flood.

Yet all around, the laughter grows,
Each cheer a punchline nature knows.
In this realm, joy takes its flight,
As we bask in the warmth of light.

Ferns and Dreams in the Tropic Night

Ferns whisper secrets to the breeze,
While iguanas chill with utter ease.
A turtle cracks a joke so grand,
As crabs parade upon the sand.

Stars twinkle like a disco ball,
While owls hoot with a comical call.
The moon's a giant, grinning face,
Illuminating this wild place.

Coconut drinks are served with flair,
While party parrots fill the air.
Bamboo beats the conga line,
As we dance under the vine.

Laughter echoes through the night,
In this paradise, pure delight.
Every moment, a joyous scene,
Where nature revels, bright and keen.

Whispers of Sunlit Canopies

Bouncing butterflies in hats so wide,
Lizards humming tunes, they cannot hide.
Parrots squawking jokes in vibrant shades,
As monkeys plan their sunny charades.

Coconuts giggle when they drop with a thud,
While iguanas slide in the playful mud.
Palm trees sway, they're quite the dancers,
Laughing at tourists and their funny glances.

Dance of the Midnight Breeze

When the moon spills milk on the sandy shore,
Crabs do the cha-cha, they always want more.
Fireflies flicker, throwing wild parties,
While sleepy frogs croak their nighttime tarts.

The stars wear shades as the wind starts to spin,
And turtles in tuxedos join in the din.
Silly shadows flit, making silly faces,
In this funny world where laughter embraces.

Coral Dreams and Sapphire Seas

Fish in bow ties swim with such grace,
While turtles float by, keeping up the pace.
Anemones giggle, tickling the dive,
In the world beneath, hilarity thrives.

A seahorse sneezes, causing ripples bright,
And dolphins do flips in the soft moonlight.
Every wave whispers a humorous tale,
As shells chuckle softly, their secrets unveil.

Echoes of Lush Vines

Vines wrapped around, a tangled ballet,
The sloths are lazy, napping all day.
While chattering monkeys swing to and fro,
They trade silly secrets we'll never know.

Bamboo giggles as it sways in delight,
And frogs play hopscotch 'neath stars shining bright.
Every branch holds laughter, hanging like fruit,
And leaves rustle softly, all in pursuit.

Echoes of Laughter in the Lagoon

The parrots squawk with all their might,
While crabs perform a dance, what a sight!
A fish in a bow tie swims with glee,
As turtles gossip just like you and me.

With coconuts bouncing, what a mess,
Sandcastles tumble, oh what distress!
Palm trees sway as if to tease,
While monkeys throw coconuts with ease.

A Celebration of Rainbow Feathers

Surfbirds roller-skate on the foam,
While sunburned tourists call this home.
A toucan giggles with hues so bright,
Telling jokes that take off in flight.

Flamingos prance in shades of pink,
With ice cream cones, they all clink!
Parrots play cards, a game of chance,
Oh, the fun of their feathered dance!

A Sunlit Poem of Waves

Waves that waltz under a shining sun,
Splashing on shore, they're having fun!
A dolphin flips, then strikes a pose,
Giggling as he tickles his toes.

Seagulls race, let's call it a game,
Chasing down the fish, oh what a claim!
Sandy shoes, what a funky style,
Watch out for crabs, they'll make you smile!

Daydreams Found Among Coral Cays

A sea turtle with shades on, so cool,
Claims the coral as his diving pool.
Starfish lounging, taking a break,
While jellyfish dance, not a mistake!

Crabs in bowler hats stroll with flair,
While fish form a band in salty air.
A pelican sings an off-key tune,
And everyone chuckles beneath the moon.

Hidden Treasures of the Island Breeze

On sandy shores, the crabs do dance,
While tourists fumble, not a chance!
With coconuts as hats, they prance,
Oh, what a sight, a funny trance!

The waves applaud, a splashy cheer,
As seagulls squawk, they steal a beer!
A treasure map, wrong turns we steer,
The island's fun is oh-so-clear!

Starlit Paths Through Blooming Night

The moonlight bathes the palm trees tall,
Where critters sing, a crazy call.
With flip-flops lost, we trip and fall,
The stars above enjoy it all!

A coconut falls, a thud! Oh dear,
A rogue mango flies, it's quite unclear!
Amidst the chaos, we shed a tear,
For laughter echoes, that's the cheer!

The Symphony of Tropical Rain

Pitter-patter on the roof, a beat,
Umbrellas up, a dance so sweet.
The rain's a band, with rhythms neat,
Splashing puddles, we skip our feet!

A parrot squawks, it joins the show,
As frogs croak loud, they steal the glow.
With every drop, our worries go,
In this wet world, we laugh, we flow!

Flavors of Sunshine and Spice

A banquet spread, so bright and wild,
With dishes named that'll make you smile.
Where tarts are tangy, each flavor styled,
It's a culinary giggle mile!

The salsa jiggles, a spicy dance,
While guavas wink, they take a chance.
With every bite, we're lost in trance,
Oh, tropical treats, let's eat, let's prance!

Swaying Horizons and Lost Comets

Under breezy palms, we stand high,
Comets lost, they wave goodbye.
Swaying like a weary dancer,
Chasing dreams, a bright romancer.

Coconuts drop with a comic thud,
As laughter echoes through the mud.
Butterflies flutter past with glee,
Trying to find their morning tea.

Nectar of the Vibrant Rainforest

Bees argue over blossoms sweet,
In this buzzing, zany retreat.
A parrot squawks, a jester's call,
Beneath the vibrant jungle wall.

Sipping nectar, all aflutter,
While monkeys throw their fruit in utter,
What a feast in colors bold,
Even the sun seems bright and old.

Crescendo of Colorful Hummingbirds

Hummingbirds zoom like restless sprites,
A race through flowers, daring heights.
With tiny beaks, they play their song,
Dodging petals all day long.

Cheeky insects join the choir,
As nature's circus climbs higher.
A grape-sized troupe of feathers whirled,
In the brightest dance this world unfurled.

Chasing the Canopy's Serenity

Treetops sway in breezy giggles,
As squirrels play with their twinkly wiggles.
Joyful shadows frolic below,
While lazy lizards take it slow.

Frogs leap high, wearing their crowns,
Crickets join with silly sounds.
All is merry, all is bright,
In this canopy, pure delight.

Beneath the Canopy of Time

Monkeys swing with grace and flair,
While parrots gossip without a care.
The sloth rolls its eyes, moves like glue,
Saying, "Why rush? Just enjoy the view!"

The jungle's a joke, nature's grand stage,
Where every leaf can steal the page.
Lizards strut in their boldest hue,
While ants march like soldiers, it's true!

Woven Tales of the Rainforest

The frogs croak a tune, a quirky choir,
While insects dance on a thread of wire.
Palm trees sway with a sassy twist,
As the breeze laughs, it simply can't resist!

Bamboo grows tall, then bends with glee,
Caught in a prank by its neighbor tree.
The sun peeks through with a cheeky grin,
Ready for mischief to begin!

The Splendor of a Distant Shore

Turtles beach-bound, on a laugh-filled stroll,
While crabs pinch toes, with a touch of control.
Seagulls squawk tales of the day before,
Daring fish to a game of hide and explore!

The waves wink softly with chortles and glee,
Inviting all creatures for tea at the sea.
With shells as their cups, and seaweed for cake,
They toast to the winds, for humor's own sake!

Revelry in the Dappled Light

Sunbeams juggle like clowns in the sky,
While shadows sneak past with a shy little sigh.
The flowers giggle, wearing bright dresses,
Allured by the humor of nature's sweet messes.

Little bugs flaunt their polka-dot suits,
While bees complain about pollen disputes.
As frogs leap and croak, it's laughter they hoard,
Under dappled light, joy is restored!

Symphony of the Coral Reefs

Beneath the waves, fish dance and twirl,
A clownfish claims its colorful world.
An octopus plots with eight-legged schemes,
While sea turtles float in their lazy dreams.

A snail in a shell tries to race a crab,
But gets sidetracked by a seaweed tab.
Coral plays tunes with a bubble's pop,
Join in the chorus; we never do stop.

A parrotfish dons its bright, silly hat,
As the anemone tickles a passing rat.
All chatter and giggles under the waves,
Each creature a comedian, nature's true knaves.

The Solstice's Sweet Embrace

The sun shines bright, what a glob of fun,
Bikini tops dancing, oh where have they run?
Flip-flops and laughter, a carnival spree,
The beach is a party, oh come join me!

A seagull swoops down, snatching a fry,
While children build castles that seem to fly.
Sunscreen is slathered, a slippery mess,
And someone just screamed, 'I've lost my dress!'

Sunsets applaud with a splash of gold,
As toes in the sand tell tales often told.
A lemonade stand runs out of its stash,
So we mix up some juice, an extravagant splash!

Dreams Beneath the Swaying Palms

Under the palms, hammock sways free,
A squirrel in sunglasses is lounging with glee.
Coconuts falling; is it time for a snack?
A monkey swings by, and it's stealing our pack!

Laughter erupts as our chips take flight,
A parrot squawks jokes, it's quite a sight.
Dreaming of treasures left buried in sand,
While crabs form a band; it's a beach rock band!

The sun starts to set, and we sing off-key,
With laughter and friendship, just you and me.
A beach bonfire crackles, as marshmallows brown,
And the stars twinkle down on our silly crown.

Firefly Flickers in Moonlit Nights

In the still of the night, a firefly parade,
Zipping about like a starry charade.
They wink at the moon, sparkly and bright,
While crickets compose, serenading the night.

A raccoon performs juggling acts on the run,
While frogs tap dance, oh isn't it fun?
They croak and they leap in a silly ballet,
Under the gaze of the moon's gentle ray.

A picnic gets raided by a family of mice,
Who take off with chips, oh, isn't that nice?
With giggles and shrieks, the night carries on,
As dreams take their flight, before the dawn.

Secrets of the Lagoon's Heart

Beneath the waves, fish try to dance,
But one fish forgot, and lost its chance.
It flipped and flopped, a watery show,
While turtles giggled, watching below.

A crab in a hat says, 'What's the deal?
I left my lunch, now how do I meal?'
The shrimp play cards by a sunken boat,
While dolphins joke, keeping it afloat.

Twilight Over Blossoming Orchards

The papaya tree wore a bright new hat,
While bees buzzed loudly, 'What of that?'
Lemons laughed, their sourness in tow,
While dancing kiwis stole the whole show!

A monkey swung low, chasing a bee,
Said, 'Buzz, buzz, I'm coming for tea!'
But tripped on a branch, oh what a sight,
As fruit friends all cheered, 'You okay, bud? Right?'

Shadows of the Coconut Grove

Beneath a palm, a lizard rehearsed,
Telling a tale that was simply the worst.
'Once I thought I could fly like a kite,
But it turns out I'm a reptile, not quite!'

Coconuts chuckled, falling with glee,
'Oh dear friend, stick to the tree!'
A parrot shrieked, 'You're quite the fool,
Maybe leave the flying to those that rule!'

Mirage in the Warmth of Paradise

A sand crab strutted with shades on tight,
Proclaiming, 'I'm cool, and ready to bite!'
But a wave came crashing, oh what a scene,
He scuttled away, not so serene!

Flamingos posed for their selfies bright,
As a clumsy one tripped—oh, what a fright!
'Next time, my friends, let's try to sway,
Without falling flat, it's just cliché!'

Melodies of the Tropical Rain

Raindrops dance on my head,
Making a hat of greens instead.
I slip and slide with every step,
Laughing at the puddles I've kept.

The frogs sing sweet little tunes,
Wearing tiny hats like cartoon raccoons.
I wish I had their rhythm and flair,
Instead, I trip on grass with my bare hair.

Palm trees sway, gossiping trees,
Sharing secrets with the wandering bees.
A coconut falls, clonk on my toe,
Now it's a fruit fight, oh what a show!

With each splash, a chuckle in sight,
As I twirl and whirl in the misty light.
In this downpour, life's quite insane,
Here's to the laughter in tropical rain!

Blossoms of the Island Breeze

The flowers giggle under the sun,
Dancing together, just having fun.
Their perfume, sweet like candy canes,
Makes you forget your earthly pains.

A parrot squawks, "Polly wants a snack!"
While I juggle fruit, it beats me back.
Coconuts rolling, it's quite the show,
Like a circus act, they steal the show!

Laughter floats on warm island air,
As I chase butterflies without a care.
They mock my runs with sudden turns,
While the sun above slowly burns.

In this breeze, we're all so spry,
With flower crowns, we touch the sky.
Life here is a merry spree,
Where joy blooms wild and carefree!

Enchantment in the Hibiscus Shade

Under hibiscus, I take my lounge,
A nap turns wild with a sneaky scrounge.
Ants march by in uniform lines,
While I dream in colors, like flowing wines.

A lizard poses, a true diva's show,
Sipping on nectar, stealing the glow.
"Hey, that's my drink!" I exclaim with glee,
He shrugs his shoulders, so carefree!

With every rustle, a secret is told,
As petals blush in pink and gold.
What's that? A wind that plays with my hair,
As if tickling me just to be fair.

Laughter bubbles like a cool stream,
Where joy peeks out from every dream.
In this shade, nothing can fade,
Just enchantment, nothing else laid!

Twilight Over Turquoise Waters

The sun dips down, a jewel to see,
The sky blushes pink, just like me!
Fish jump high, with splashes and spins,
While seagulls steal my crispy chips wins.

The waves chuckle at the shore,
As I build castles that topple galore.
"Oops!" echoes through the evening bliss,
As I step back just to catch a kiss.

Stars peek out, playing hide and seek,
While the moon winks at my silly streak.
I dance with shadows, twirling around,
As laughter dances, joy abounds.

In twilight's glow, stories unfold,
With each chuckle, my spirit bold.
Here in the magic, fun reigns supreme,
A playful world born from every dream!

Canvas of the Setting Sun

Crayons melting on the shore,
Palms waving as they roar.
Sandy toes and jellyfish,
Tiki torches and a swish!

Seagulls squawking like a band,
As they steal my hotdog stand.
Flip-flops flapping, what a scene,
Coconuts roll, I'm feeling mean!

Sunsets that paint the skies in gold,
Mermaids laughing, oh so bold.
Forget my worries, toss them away,
I'll bring a surfboard—who needs a bouquet?

Painting dreams upon the sand,
With each wave, I take a stand.
Dancing mermaids twirl and sway,
Let's have fun, it's time to play!

Kisses of a Golden Horizon

Waves that giggle as they crash,
Turtles dancing with a splash.
Sunshine melts the ice cream cone,
A sweet delight, all on my own.

Dolphins leap like acrobats,
Stealing my last crumb of snacks.
Golden rays that tickle skin,
Time to dive and take a spin!

Palm trees chatter in the breeze,
Spinning tales with such great ease.
Laughter bubbles from the sea,
Join the dance, come sail with me!

As the starfish do the twist,
Don't you dare forget the mist!
With every sunset, life's a show,
In this paradise, let the good times flow!

Swaying Hearts by the Water's Edge

Couples jiving on the sand,
Trying hard to hold a hand.
Grass skirts flying round and round,
Tripping on this merry ground.

Crabs are marching in a line,
Honking horns, they're feeling fine.
The music plays, the fire starts,
We sway and dance with all our hearts.

Fish are diving in the blue,
As I try to impress you.
But I slipped and fell with a clap,
The ocean is now my lap!

Under stars so bright and clear,
These funny moments, let's hold dear.
With laughter echoing through the night,
We'll keep dancing till first light!

Breathing in the Island Air

Gentle breezes tease my hair,
Warm embraces, light as air.
Sunscreen dances on my nose,
As my laughter comes and goes.

Lunch is served, we share a bite,
Tropical fruits feeling just right.
But watch out for the sneaky bee,
You take the honey, I'll take the tea!

Every moment wrapped in glee,
Fishes winking back at me.
Jokes flow like the ocean tide,
With every wave, we take a ride.

So here's to fun, let the day unfold,
In this paradise, our lives are bold.
With every breeze, our spirits soar,
Let's laugh together, forevermore!

Blossoms on a Windswept Path

Petals dance like little clowns,
Their laughter swirls through sunny towns.
Breezes tease my floppy hat,
Chasing me like a playful cat.

Butterflies wear tiny shoes,
As they frolic, spreading news.
Flowers giggle, colors bright,
Waving at the sunlight's bite.

I trip over roots and twigs,
Swaying like a feathered jig.
Nature's jokes are everywhere,
Giggling clouds in the warm air.

With every step, a silly hum,
Tropical beats make me feel numb.
Oh, the joy of this wild spree,
Where laughter grows on every tree.

Resplendent Moments on Sandy Shores

Sandy toes and seaweed hair,
Crabs crab-walk with perfect flair.
Seagulls squawk their witty lines,
While I struggle to draw straight lines.

Beach balls bounce with cheeky laughs,
As sunburnt faces tell their gaffes.
The ocean's jokes come in waves,
Tickling our toes in watery graves.

Sandcastles rise like royal plans,
Only to fall to playful hands.
Children giggle, the tide comes in,
Splashing them from chin to chin.

A sun hat flies, caught by a breeze,
I flail and laugh, oh, what a tease!
Moments here are never drab,
Life's a beach with laughter to grab.

Tides of Laughter and Lament

Waves crash down, a slapstick show,
Dancing crabs steal the spotlight's glow.
Shells giggle as they're tossed aside,
Pretending they're on a rollercoaster ride.

The sun smiles, but don't be fooled,
It turns our backs to tacos schooled.
Seashells whisper tales so grand,
Of fortunes lost on this sandy land.

Fishermen pull off cheeky pranks,
Reeling in seaweed, not fish, in flanks.
A mermaid flips her tail with glee,
As I trip over her soap-sudded spree.

The tide comes in, brings funny tides,
Joking with us, as it abides.
In the depths, laughter fills the air,
Tides whirl by with playful flair.

The Warmth Beneath the Banana Leaves

Beneath green canopies so bright,
Monkey giggles take flight.
Bananas wear their peels like hats,
Swinging with the chittering chats.

Sunbeams poke through leafy roofs,
As I trip on nature's goofs.
Bugs create a buzzing choir,
Singing tunes that never tire.

Each shadow tells a funny tale,
Of lizards on a slippery scale.
The jungle roars with laughter loud,
While I stumble, feeling proud.

Palm trees wave a silly dance,
In this wacky, playful prance.
Underneath these leafy fans,
Life's a joke—bring on the plans!

A Rhapsody of Coconut Serenades

Coconuts dance on the swaying trees,
With every breeze, they tease and please.
A coconut fell, and oh what a sound,
A laugh from the beach, joy all around.

A parrot squawks, trying to sing,
But misses the tune, what a funny thing!
Shells play maracas as crabs keep the beat,
A calypso of critters, a tropical treat.

Sunhats and sunglasses, a fashion parade,
While flip-flops trip on the sun-baked glade.
Laughter erupts as a toddler slips,
In a puddle of laughter, a perfect eclipse.

With rum in a cup, our spirits are high,
As lizards join in, oh me, oh my!
The rhythm of joy in this sandy retreat,
Is one that you'll cherish, a rhythm so sweet.

Between the Glistening Shores

Between the waves, the sunbeams splash,
Seagulls squawk, with a comical crash.
Sandcastles rise, but the tide has its say,
As a wave topples kingdoms in a playful display.

Beach balls soar like funny balloons,
While sunscreen battles against the noons.
A group of tourists with hats too wide,
Searching for shade like it's a wild ride.

Ice cream drips, as laughter rings loud,
Melting away, they all feel quite proud.
But a seagull swoops, with a sly little glance,
Snatching a cone, what a daring chance!

Sunsets blaze, painting skies with cheer,
As friends pass a joke over their beer.
With each chuckle, the night softly calls,
Echoes of laughter, where joy never falls.

Glistening Paths Through the Oasis

Winding paths edged with colors bright,
Where lizards dash, giving quite the fright.
A monkey swings, with a cheeky grin,
At the moment when laughter begins!

Palm fronds wave as if to say,
"Join the party, come out and play!"
A puddle reflects a crazy dance,
As sandals splash in a glimmering trance.

Mangoes roll down, what a slippery feat,
While belly laughs echo, a joyful heartbeat.
Under the shade, with drinks piled high,
We toast to the tropics, oh me, oh my!

The sun dips low, hues bright in the sky,
As fireflies twinkle, they flit and fly.
Hands in the air, we celebrate bliss,
In laughter and song, we find our sweet kiss.

The Harmony of the Jungle's Breath

In the jungle's heart, where the wild things play,
A toucan sports colors, oh what a display!
With each loud honk and a gleeful screech,
The fun of the forest is within easy reach.

Vines twist like dancers in a vibrant ball,
While frogs croak melodies, both big and small.
A tiger naps, dreaming of fish,
But wakes with a start, quite the funny wish!

Swaying to rhythms of insects' hum,
A tribe of chipmunks all dance to the drum.
Under the leaves, laughter does swell,
As a squirrel steals snacks, what a mischievous spell!

The sun peeks through, casting gold on the floor,
With giggles echoing forevermore.
As the jungle breathes, a giggle we find,
In nature's embrace, we leave worries behind.

Serenade of the Sand

Oh, the grainy beach, what a treat,
Sandy toes dance to the sun's beat.
Crabs in tuxedos scuttle around,
In this sandy shindig, there's joy unbound.

Laughter echoes, waves crash near,
Beach balls soar, and then disappear.
With sunscreen slathered like a coat,
We glide on surfboards, or just float.

Seagulls squawk, they're quite the show,
Stealing fries, oh, that's their flow.
Life's a picnic, sunburned and bright,
With ice cream drips, what a delight!

So let's toast to the sandy bliss,
With coconut drinks and a splashy kiss.
Here's to the fun we will not lose,
In our silly sunny beachy news.

Vibrant Vistas of Verdant Isles

Green leaves flutter, what a sight,
Lizards sunbathe, oh what a bite!
Coconuts fall, a thud like the beat,
As monkeys swing, this day can't be beat.

Bananas are ripe, and so full of cheer,
But watch out, they'll disappear near.
Swaying grass sings a funny tune,
While twerking trees dance under the moon.

The parrots squawk, think they're so slick,
But mischief brews, it's their little trick.
A toucan sneezes, with colors so bright,
In this jungle gym, it's pure delight.

So grab a hammock, take a rest,
These vibrant sights, they are the best.
With a wink and a smile, we'll roam this isle,
With all things green, let's stay awhile.

Tides of Lush Serenity

Waves whisper secrets on the shore,
While fish jump up and dance for more.
Snorkels sparkling with laughter and glee,
Who knew the ocean could be so free?

Floating in pools of blue and green,
Life's a splash zone, a jovial scene.
With floaties on, we look quite absurd,
As we paddle by, all laughter stirred.

The sea turtles just shake their heads,
While we trip over our colorful threads.
Seashells giggle, with stories to tell,
Of amusing swims and waves that fell.

So let the tides take us far and wide,
On this aquatic circus, let's take a ride.
With a splash and a cheer, our journey's complete,
In this water world, oh what a feat!

Twilight Kiss of the Palm Leaves

Palm trees sway as daylight dips,
Kissing the horizon with sunset tips.
Cocktails clink under a pink sky,
While fireflies kiss the air, oh my!

Chasing shadows, we laugh and spin,
As the evening's glow draws us in.
Flip-flops flopping with each silly step,
In the dance of the night, we misrep.

The stars arrive, a twinkling crew,
But watch out for those drinks, they'll pursue!
A tropical breeze, tickles our face,
In this nighttime fun, we find our place.

So let's raise our glasses to the night,
With laughter and cheer, everything feels right.
In the glow of the moon, we'll sing and play,
As palm leaves sway, let's dance away.

Soft Footfalls on Woven Sands

Sandy toes and silly hats,
Frolicking with sun-baked cats,
The crabs do waltz, while we just dance,
In this realm of sun-kissed chance.

Flip-flops squeak with every step,
While seagulls eye our snacks, they prep,
We chase the waves, they chase our chips,
In silly swimsuits, we take our dips.

Tents are flapping, mops on heads,
We try to nap but roll in beds,
With sunscreen splatters, laughter loud,
A sunburned spirit, oh so proud.

This paradise, a joyful site,
Sandy pranks from morn to night,
Woven tales of laughter shared,
Of flip-flops lost and fun declared.

Serengeti of the Southern Skies

A lion's roar, oh what a joke,
It's just my friend who drooled and choked,
While zebras play in stripes of glee,
We snack on bananas, wild and free.

The sun dips low, we set our sights,
On dancing ants and starry nights,
With belly laughs, the rhinos snort,
In this wild land, we have our sport.

My dance moves make the monkeys stare,
While alligators just don't care,
We trek through jungles, bright and bold,
With tales of wonder yet untold.

Underneath the twinkling lights,
We wear our crowns, like noble knights,
Laughing at the jesters here,
In this vast land, we have no fear.

Whispers of the Sunlit Shore

Where palm trees sway and giggles rise,
The ocean whispers silly lies,
Octopuses throwing confetti high,
While mermaids grin from the sapphire sky.

With beach balls bouncing, kids collide,
Our laughter echoing like a tide,
In towel capes, we strut with grace,
While seagulls join our wobbly race.

Sandcastles crumble while we cheer,
As waves embrace with playful sneer,
The sun dips low, we yell 'Hooray!'
For sand-sculptured dreams at the end of day.

But wait, what's that? A crab on sand!
Running from the beach's grand band,
In the warmth of this timeless quest,
Joyful chaos, we are truly blessed.

Laughter of the Caribbean Breeze

The breeze is high; the jokes flow free,
We play hide-and-seek with coconut trees,
Mango mush on everyone's face,
In this paradise, we find our place.

The roaches dance at the midnight feast,
While iguanas groove, we drink the least,
The salsa rhythms make us thrill,
Swirling short shorts, up and down the hill.

With a flip and a flop, we dive right in,
Splashing water all over our skin,
As jellyfish float; we cry 'Not me!'
The ocean's whims, oh so carefree.

Later we feast on grilled fish bites,
Chasing laughter under moonlit nights,
With jokes that echo across the seas,
Our hearts are light in this gentle breeze.

Paintbrush of the Ocean's Edge

A crab in shades of pink,
Dances on the shore, I think.
He slips on seaweed, takes a fall,
Then flips back up, a true sea stall.

The waves giggle, oh so bright,
Making fish wear hats of light.
Seashells whisper secrets old,
While sunburnt seagulls scold and scold.

Sandcastles melt without a care,
A royal moat, oh what a scare!
As tides come in with thunderous glee,
And knock the kingdom down with glee.

Yet laughter echoes in the breeze,
As jellyfish do the cha-cha tease.
In this art of salty fun,
We laugh and play, we've just begun!

An Oasis of Unraveled Dreams

Palm trees wave, they dance with flair,
While monkeys steal my sunhat rare.
They wear it like a crown of pride,
And swing from dreams where wishes hide.

Lizards lounge in shades so cool,
They lay claim to the kiddie pool.
With tiny shades and fruit drinks near,
They're the guests who never steered.

A parrot squawks a tune off-key,
And sings of love, oh woe is me!
With feathers flying, quite a show,
Each note deserves a big "Oh no!"

Yet in this space where laughter beams,
We find the craziest of dreams.
With mirage-swirled jokes and gleams,
We chuckle here, or so it seems.

Whirlwind of Fragrant Petals

The flowers dance in breezy craze,
Like fashion models, set ablaze.
Each petal twirls in rhyme and cheer,
As gnomes join in with laughter clear.

A bee in shades buzzes around,
Trying to find the sweetest sound.
It bumps into a flower's face,
And off it goes in quite a race.

A pup digs holes, oh what a sight,
He brings out treasures from the night.
With dirt-stained paws and cheeky bark,
He finds a shoe—just what a lark!

Yet petals fall like candy sprinkles,
As laughter grows, and joy just crinkles.
In this whirlwind of sweet perfume,
We dance till dusk, banish the gloom!

Sun-Kissed Sanctuary of Miracles

The sun rolls out its golden bed,
While flip-flops hop around, well-led.
A cat joins in, purring with pride,
A sunny throne, her joy to ride.

A picnic spread, oh what a feast,
With ants parade, a marching beast.
They steal the crumbs with little grace,
And turn a snack into a race.

The ice cream melts upon our hands,
While giggles burst like happy bands.
A cone slips down, a sticky flare,
We laugh because we truly care.

So here's to joy in every ray,
As laughter brightens up our play.
In this refuge of simple fun,
We dance until the day is done!

Delights of the Spice-scented Air

There's a parrot who thinks he can dance,
Wobbling around in his bright feathered pants.
He twirls and he leaps, with a flapping delight,
While the mangoes just roll, oh what a sight!

The palms bend with laughter, what a funny show,
As a monkey grabs coconuts, ready to throw.
He tosses them high, they go smashing so sweet,
While the iguanas watch, with their feet on their feet.

A lizard on the branch takes a daring dive,
Into the lemonade pitcher, feels so alive!
The kids laugh and giggle, they cheer with such glee,
As their drink turns into a spurting spree.

In the end, as the sun starts to sink,
The critters gather, with a wink and a blink.
They toast to the chaos, with laughter and cheer,
In this spice-scented world, we're all welcome here!

The Cradle of the Wild Tropics

In the wild where the monkeys wear shades and get tan,
   They sip on their smoothies, it's all part of the plan.
   With a swing and a flip, they prank every fool,
   While a toucan just laughs, such a colorful tool!

A sloth wearing flip-flops just chillaxin' out back,
   Dining on figs, while he's lost on the track.
   He dreams of a sprint, but it's quite a big feat,
   So he'll stay dangling, enjoying the heat.

With a wink and a nod, the chameleons tease,
Changing colors for fun, like a breeze in the trees.
At the dance-off tonight, they'll steal every show,
   As the fireflies twinkle in a dazzling glow.

Each critter joins in, all with silly flair,
   In a raucous ballet, they twirl through the air.
   It's a chorus of giggles, a harmony bright,
In this cradle of wild, we laugh through the night!

Footprints in the Soft White Sands

There are footprints in sand, but what do they mean?
Was it a crab in disguise, or a chicken who's keen?
They shuffle and hop, as they make quite a scene,
While the breeze starts to whistle, a comical theme.

A turtle beside them, moves at slow motion,
As he dreams of a race against an ocean's potion.
The gulls start to cackle, as he takes a deep breath,
While the waves gently giggle, like it's all just a jest.

A beach ball gets tossed, oh, it's flying so high,
It lands on a bear who's just passing by.
With a snort and a roll, he tries to take aim,
And then back to the ocean, he shuffles in shame.

As the sun bows low, with a wink and a glow,
The secrets of footprints, they'll never quite know.
In this land full of laughter, so carefree and grand,
We map out our fun, with our toes in the sand!

The Song of the Nightingale's Nest

There's a nightingale perched in a tree way up high,
Singing funny rhymes that will make your heart fly.
With a croak and a squawk, he tells tales so wild,
Of a fish who would giggle, a humorous child.

The breeze carries tunes, like a breeze that can dance,
As the frogs play their drums, all part of the chance.
They ribbit and hop, adding beats to the song,
While the stars start to twinkle, joining along.

The night glimmers bright, with a laughter parade,
As the fireflies swirl, in a shimmering cascade.
Each melody sweet, brings a smile to each face,
In this comedic concert, all creatures embrace.

With a sigh and a chuckle, the moon glows so near,
As the nightingale sings, with a giggle sincere.
In the branches above, joy's nest is alive,
With the sound of our laughter, it truly can thrive!

Whispers of the Waterfall's Song

The waterfall sings with glee,
Fish dance like they're on spree.
Loud frogs croak a quirky cheer,
While monkeys swing from branch to sphere.

Splashing droplets, a playful game,
A parrot swoops, calls my name.
Bananas flying, what a sight,
As I dodge with all my might.

Lizards laugh, sunbathing bright,
A turtle sneezes, what a fright!
The breeze whispers silly clues,
While crickets wear their dancing shoes.

Under shadows where palm trees sway,
I join the fun, then slip away.
The laughter echoes through the mist,
In this wild world, I can't resist.

The Color of Tropical Blood

In this land, we wear our hues,
Mango orange, vibrant blues.
Limes and lemons draw a grin,
Even coconuts join in the din.

Parrots squabble, feathers bright,
A grasshopper hops with delight.
Flamingos pose like champs on shore,
Making every passerby implore.

The air is thick with jokes and fun,
Under the blazing, blazing sun.
A piña colada spills on the ground,
And everyone laughs, what a sound!

We paint the town with fruits so bold,
Every moment, a tale retold.
In this canvas, wild and free,
The color of joy is all we see.

Rays of Hope in a Fragrant Garden

In the garden, scents collide,
Giggling blooms, they cannot hide.
Roses tell secrets to the breeze,
While daisies dance with mischievous ease.

Sunlight tickles every leaf,
Bees and butterflies share a brief.
A chubby rabbit, what a sight,
Nibbles petals with pure delight.

Citrus and mint fill the air,
While ants march with a little flair.
The tomatoes blush, oh so red,
As a sleepy cat takes a spread.

In this patch, laughter sprouts,
Nothing's serious, no doubts.
Nature knows the funniest tricks,
With every petal, my spirit ticks.

Under the Watchful Eye of the Parrots

High above, with vibrant views,
Parrots gossip, share the news.
One claims to have met a snail,
That told tales of wind and sail.

They squawk in colors, bright and clear,
While I sip my drink with cheer.
A toucan drops a fruit so round,
And everyone laughs at the sound.

Under branches, shadows play,
As monkeys plot their next ballet.
Laughter bounces, fills the air,
Nature's jesters everywhere.

In this circus, wild and spry,
Where birds and trees reach for the sky.
With every chortle, every squawk,
Life becomes a quirky talk.

Whims of the Tropical Winds

The breeze tickles my nose, a ticklish tease,
It plays with my hat, oh where's that breeze?
Palm trees dancing, oh what a sight,
As coconuts fall, it gives me a fright.

Sandy toes are now peeking out,
While crabs are scuttling, without a doubt.
Sipping from coconuts, feeling so fine,
Just hope this sun doesn't turn me to brine.

The parrots squawk in comedic delight,
They chuckle at me, what a funny sight!
A flip-flop flings off, it flies with glee,
While I chase it down, just like a bee.

The winds swirl and spin, and I'm caught in play,
I spin like a top in the sun's bright ray.
With laughter and joy, I dance with the beams,
In this tropical jest, where life's just a dream.

A Ballet of Living Colors

The flowers bloom in a vibrant show,
While bees buzz around, like they're in the know.
A flamingo prances, doing a jig,
While I trip in the hammock, oh what a big gig!

Bananas swing low, like they're in a race,
While monkeys applaud, they're keeping the pace.
Mangoes fall down with a splat and a splash,
As I slip on a peel, oh what a crash!

Islanders laugh, sharing tales on the shore,
With fish in the net, they barter and score.
The sunset a canvas painted so bright,
Sunscreen on noses, what a comical sight!

As I twirl with joy, feeling weightless and bold,
This dance of the colors, a story retold.
With laughter and whimsy, we celebrate free,
In this ballet of life, just you wait and see.

The Horizon's Whispering Sea

The waves giggle softly, tickling the shore,
While I lay on my towel, trying to snore.
Seagulls swoop down to steal my lunch,
I shout, "Hey! That's my sandwich!" What a punch!

A hermit crab puffs up, putting on airs,
While I laugh at its stance, it just seems unfair.
The sea whispers secrets, tickling my ear,
With every splash sounding like a cheer!

The fishermen laugh as they cast out their lines,
Catching fish that wriggle and perform funny signs.
I join in their banter, trying to reel,
But only catch seaweed—a slippery meal!

As the horizon blushes, painting the skies,
I wave at the sunset, it winks with its eyes.
In this comedic play, the sea sets the stage,
With laughter and waves, we turn a new page.

Embrace of the Island's Pulse

The drums beat loudly, like a wild heart,
And I dance like nobody, in my own quirky part.
With each little shimmy, the island does cheer,
As I trip over toes, but I've got no fear!

The night sparkles bright with stars all aglow,
While the lizards do cartwheels, putting on a show.
The fireflies flicker, like they know the beat,
As I whirl around them, feeling the heat!

With friends gathered 'round, the smiles grow wide,
We share silly stories, bursting with pride.
With each tropical breeze, we roll with the jest,
In the pulse of the island, we're truly blessed.

So let's laugh 'til we cry, beneath the moonbeam,
As the rhythm of paradise fuels each silly dream.
In this embrace of joy, we twirl and we sway,
With laughter and love, we'll dance the night away.

Where the Fruit Trees Meet the Sea

Coconuts dance with the breeze,
Mangoes fall like jellybeans,
A parrot laughs over tea,
As I chase my runaway dreams.

The sand is sticky with delight,
As my flip-flops take flight,
Pineapples join the parade,
While sunburned noses are made.

A crab wears a tiny crown,
Judging all from its sandy throne,
A beach ball bounces with glee,
In a world of fruit and sea.

So here on this sunny shore,
Life's a joke given more!
Laughter mingles with the brine,
As I sip my drink divine.

Shadows on a Golden Beach

Umbrellas tilt like tipsy hats,
Sunscreen slings and silly chats,
Seagulls steal my crispy fries,
While tourists wear their tan disguise.

My buddy's tan was quite the tale,
A lobster now, he cannot fail!
As shadows stretch and giggles flow,
We pose for pics just to show.

Footprints lead to nowhere fast,
While laughter echoes, unsurpassed,
Bare toes buried in the fluff,
This beach life is more than enough.

As night falls, we share our dreams,
Understars that wink and beam,
Life's absurdity, sweet and deep,
On this golden beach, we leap.

Beyond the Horizon's Embrace

The ocean's grin is wide and bright,
As dolphins join the merry flight,
My sunscreen smells like coconut pie,
While I ponder if I can fly.

The sunset twerks on the water's edge,
As I sit on my sandy ledge,
With a drink that's far too sweet,
I toast to daydreams, what a treat!

Fish wear tiny sunglasses cool,
Making waves, they rule the pool,
I chuckle at their splashy games,
As mermaids shout some silly names.

Tomorrow holds more sunlit fun,
Adventure waits for everyone,
With each new wave that rolls ashore,
The laughter echoes, forever more.

Flickers of Paradise

Fireflies dance in twilight's glow,
While I chase shadows, to and fro,
My hat's too big, it hides my cheer,
As crickets chirp their night-time beer.

The palm trees sway in silly style,
With vine-like laughter all the while,
I stumble on the sandy spit,
But find myself laughing, not a bit!

A raccoon steals my midnight snack,
With a swift and sneaky little hack,
As stars bathe us in diamond dust,
We share our foolish tales, we must.

In this paradise where giggles roam,
I realize I've found my home,
So here's to laughter twinkling bright,
Under jolly moonbeams' light.

Dance of the Treetop Shadows

Leaves shimmy and shake, doing the twist,
Lizards join in, none can resist.
Monkeys swing low, with giggles galore,
While parrots squawk out, "Dance more and more!"

The branches all sway, a natural show,
Local critters join in, stealing the glow.
Bouncing like popcorn, the whole forest sways,
A leafy parade that brightens our days!

From the tallest of palms to the ground,
Even the ants have their own dance round.
Each creature in rhythm, it's truly a sight,
Nighttime comes on, but the fun's just right!

As shadows grow long, they twirl and they spin,
A carnival joy, no need for a win!
The dance might be silly, but oh what a thrill,
In this twisted party, we laugh and we chill!

Kinetics of the Coastal Breeze

The winds like to play, with a cheeky little jest,
Tickling my toes, putting sand on my vest.
Seagulls are laughing, they swoop down to tease,
While shells roll away, caught up in the breeze!

Palm trees are swaying, they're part of the fun,
Doing the fandango under the sun.
A crab takes a bow, with a wink and a grin,
This beach scene is wild– let the games begin!

Flip-flops are flying, and someone takes chase,
Chasing their footwear at an awkward pace.
The surf starts to bubble, then crashes with glee,
As waves clap their hands, "Come laugh with me!"

Along the shore's edge, the sandcastles rise,
But watch for the tide; it wears a sly guise.
A splash and a splatter, watch kingdoms fall down,
Yet we cheer and we giggle, as we paddle around!

Reflections in Jade Waters

The water's so green, it makes me just laugh,
Is that a fish or one silly giraffe?
I squint and I ponder, while floating in bliss,
A mermaid or two might just give me a kiss!

Waves ripple like laughter, oh what a sight,
They tickle the shore, then take off in flight.
A dolphin does cartwheels, a big splashy show,
While my float drifts away – oh no, not the flow!

The reflections are funny, they dance as they please,
A flip-flopping fin, with a wink at the trees.
Giggles from minnows, as they prance in their school,
In water so jade, we'll swim like a fool!

Twilight starts to creep, but the chuckles won't cease,
Even as day fades, we find our release.
"Last one to shore wears a crown made of sea!"
Oh, life in the water, just too funny to flee!

The Call of the Island Fables

Once upon a time, or so the tale goes,
There lived a wise turtle, who spoke with his toes.
His stories were wild, gave all of us grins,
About conch shells that danced and the laughter of fins!

A crab claimed a throne made of driftwood and sand,
Said, "Join me for tea, it's quite grand!"
But tea turned to laughter, as cups flew away,
And the crab, well, he giggled, through the chaos at play.

The parrots recite tales from the high palm trees,
Each whistled note drips with giggle-filled teas.
The animals gather, in the cool evening light,
Sharing fables of mischief that lasted all night!

As moonlight dizzies the trees with a glow,
Every critter is dancing, putting on a show.
So here's to the fables, both funny and bright,
In the heart of the isle, where laughter takes flight!

Dance of the Coconut Palms

Coconuts sway in a breeze,
Dancing lightly with great ease.
One took a fall, oh what a sight,
Rolling fast, it gave a fright!

Ripe and ready for a snack,
A crab scuttles, no time to slack.
"Don't you dare!" a parrot squawks,
"That's my dinner, I'll call the cops!"

Tourists laugh at this bright show,
As sunbeams dance, they come and go.
With each twist, a story shared,
Of frizzy hair and sunburned dared!

In this land where laughter grows,
Under palms, the fun just flows.
So join the dance, embrace the fun,
In this place, we all are one!

Secrets Harbored in Sunlit Coves

Beneath the waves, a treasure lies,
Among the fish, a crab in disguise.
It wears a hat, quite out of place,
Sent off in style, with crustacean grace.

Seagulls gossip from their perch,
Whispers of fish who failed to lurch.
"Oh look," one says with a haughty smile,
"That's the fisherman, he's tied up a while!"

The sun-drenched sands, a laughter track,
Kids build castles, but they lack!
A wave crashes, down comes the fort,
The tide's a bully, of that, we report.

Secrets kept in every shell,
In this cove, all secrets dwell.
With giggles echoing, waves in chase,
Where laughter brightens every face!

The Taste of Sweet Pineapple Dreams

Juicy wedges on the plate,
Sipping drinks, oh it's just great!
A lady slips, her drink in flight,
Still she laughs, what a funny sight!

"Who knew pineapples could bounce?" she said,
As fruit rolled away—oh what a spread!
"Do they run?" a child did ask,
With giggles loud, they took to task.

Hula dancers whirl all around,
Fruits become the stage, we've found.
Pineapples prance, tiptoeing on toes,
In a fruity ballet that surely glows.

Taste buds tingling, laughter loud,
In this feast, we're all so proud.
For sweetness flows in each embrace,
With fruity dreams, we find our place!

Journey Through Emerald Trails

On emerald paths, socks on our feet,
We march along, what a funny feat!
A lizard darts, causing a shout,
"Oh watch your step!" as we twist about.

With every curve, a giggling spree,
"Did you see that?" Two birds in a tree.
One wears a hat, such fashion flair,
While the other frets, "It's not fair!"

We stumble upon a hidden brook,
Froggie croaks, with quite the look.
"Do you laugh?" he asks, with a grin,
"I've seen worse, so let's begin!"

Emerald trails lead us to cheer,
With nature's jokes ringing clear.
In this journey, we find our bliss,
With laughter sweet, who'd want to miss?

Dancers Beneath the Mango Trees

Mangoes fall like splashes of sun,
The dancers grin, their fun just begun.
Little feet, they twirl and prance,
While mango flies lead the vibrant dance.

A parrot caws, thinks he's the best,
But his moves, oh dear, fail the test.
Lemons roll, it's quite the scene,
While laughter bursts like a bright green bean.

Bongo drums beat with a funky vibe,
Swaying hips catch that fruity jibe.
Caught in the rhythm, they carelessly sway,
As the sun spills laughter in a tropical way.

With a splash of lemonade on their face,
They jive and giggle with such sweet grace.
Mango trees laugh, swaying with ease,
As nature joins in for this wild jamboree.

Echoes of the Ocean's Heart

Waves crash dancing, a slippery show,
Seagulls squawk, putting on a tow.
Shells wear grins, as crabs take a crack,
They pinch each other, then scuttle back.

Surfboards tumble like fish out of school,
Riders yell, 'Dude, this ain't so cool!'
Splashing waves, a slippery race,
As dolphins giggle, their smiles in place.

Sunburnt tourists trying to glide,
With beach balls bouncing to take them for a ride.
Sunscreen mishaps and hot sand burns,
Echoes of laughter with every churn.

Fishes gossip, sharing the tide,
As shells conspire, oh what a ride!
The ocean's heart beats wild and free,
While silly beach games create such glee.

Secrets of the Coconut Grove

Coconuts hide the strangest tales,
Of coconut crabs in giant pails.
A squirrel sneaks, with a look so sly,
Swiping lunch, oh my oh my!

Palm trees chuckle, twist with flair,
While wind whispers, 'Do you dare?'
The groves hold secrets in their sway,
As monkeys throw ripe nuts all day.

Coconuts tumble, a clumsy ballet,
While lazy lizards sunbathe all day.
The ground's a stage, nature's delight,
In a comedy show from morning to night.

Breezes carry a giggle or two,
As the grove hums a playful tune.
With each rustle, the laughter flows,
In this secret space where humor grows.

Hummingbirds at Dusk

Hummingbirds zoom in a dizzying flight,
With beaks like straws sipping nectar bright.
Tiny legends with feathers so fine,
They flash their jewels, 'Come join our line!'

Flowers giggle, tickled by their speed,
As petals sway to the dancer's creed.
A bee gives chase, but misses the cue,
While laughing blooms shout, 'We see you!'

At dusk they'll taste the sweetest delights,
Mystic flavors in the fading lights.
With each buzz, a raucous cheer,
As they twirl around, spreading cheer.

So let the nightfall guide their spin,
With nature's laughter, they dance and grin.
In tiny forms, the humor unfolds,
In every loop, a tale retold.

Serenade Under the Palm Fronds

Beneath the fronds we dance so wild,
Our moves a mix of grace and child.
A coconut drops, we slip and fall,
Laughter echoes, a joyful call.

The parrot sings a silly tune,
We join along, our voices croon.
A crab walks by, with sideways flair,
Who knew beach critters had such care?

We sip cocktails, umbrellas bright,
A toast to days that feel just right.
The sun dips low, a balmy breeze,
As we perform for golden seas.

Under stars, our antics bloom,
A twirl, a spin, we fill the room.
Sand in our shorts, we laugh and shout,
Who knew the beach could bring such clout?

Luminous Dusk on Sandy Shores

The sun reduces to a ball,
And seafoam whispers, 'Watch your fall!'
A seagull swoops, it steals my fry,
I chase it down with a silly cry.

A limbo game, we bend so low,
The palm trees giggle at our show.
But oh! My back, it creaks and moans,
This limbo's tougher than my bones!

We spot a crab, with such a stance,
It seems more poised than us in dance.
"Take notes," I say, "it's quite the sight!"
We break into laughter, what a night!

The stars come out, a winking light,
Our goofy moves still feel so right.
With laughter echoing through the night,
We cherish moments, pure delight.

Tropical Rain's Soft Embrace

Dancing droplets on my nose,
A sudden shower, and there it goes!
We dash for cover, a nearby shed,
Where laughter comes instead of dread.

The storm makes waves, a splashing game,
I slip and slide, no one's to blame.
A rainbow forms, we squeal with glee,
Dancing in puddles, oh, let it be!

Wet hair and smiles, laughter floods,
Our fashion's high, in muddy thuds.
Who needs a spa? We're drenched in fun,
The sun will shine when the rain is done.

So toast the rain, this playful host,
With every splash, we laugh the most.
The soft embrace of stormy play,
Makes memories bright, come what may!

Breathe of the Emerald Rainforest

Underneath the canopy wide,
A monkey swings, with such great pride.
I trip on roots, I take a dive,
The jungle laughs, I feel alive.

Vines in the trees, like hair gone wild,
Leaves tango down, the forest's child.
A toucan squawks, "Make way for me!"
As I twirl like it's a jubilee.

A frog jumps in, that pesky chap,
He steals my shoe, and I yelp, "Snap!"
The flora grins, it's just pure fun,
In this green maze, we all are one.

So embrace the chaos, don't you see?
The rainforest calls, "Come laugh with me!"
With every step, a tale unfolds,
In emerald hues, our joy consoles.

Voices of the Gentle Waves

Laughter skips on salty air,
Seagulls chat without a care.
Sandcastles lean, a bit askew,
As children squeal, their joy in view.

Palm trees sway with carefree glee,
While coconuts drop, just wait and see.
Beach towels spread like colorful wings,
As laughter bursts, oh how it sings!

Waves roll in, tickling toes,
While sunburns bloom on funny nose.
Ice cream drips, a sticky treat,
As sand finds homes in every seat.

Shells are treasures, crabs a joke,
They scuttle quick with a little poke.
In this paradise, we all unite,
For silly moments bathed in light.

Pathways of Golden Flickers

Sunbeams dance on ocean's glint,
Flip-flops flop, what a hint!
Kids chase shadows, giggles ring,
As flip-flops launch, oh what a fling!

A parrot squawks with what it thinks,
While folks are busy grabbing drinks.
Sunscreen flies like sticky confetti,
While laughter bubbles, oh so petty.

Surfboards tumble in the surf,
As dolphins dive, they claim their turf.
Beach balls bounce, and laughter spills,
Creating joy that simply thrills.

Sunsets melt in colors bright,
With jokes shared well into the night.
The moon will join the jest, oh dear,
In this paradise, we shed a tear!

Tides of Cerulean Reflections

Waves giggle as they crash and play,
With sandy feet, we dance all day.
Crab races start, oh what a scene,
With little legs, so swift and keen.

Bikinis bright, a comedic sight,
As we strut and sashay, oh what a delight!
Cool drinks spill with a hearty cheer,
While waves applaud, they're always near.

Seashells whisper silly rhymes,
While laughter echoes through the climbs.
Beach umbrellas, colorful caps,
Hide secrets of our wacky laps.

Sunburned cheeks and glowing grins,
Mark the ends where mischief begins.
Each night a show, with stars our props,
Oh how the fun, it never stops!

Journey Through Vivid Horizons

Tropical breeze, a chuckle found,
As kite strings tangle on the ground.
Flip-flops dance, a silly race,
While laughter spills all over the place.

Clouds Skittering, like playful sheep,
While kids dive into waters deep.
Banana peels just waiting there,
For unsuspecting feet to dare.

Crabs in suits, oh what a sight,
Strutting sideways, in sheer delight.
A tournament of sand-clad knights,
As we defend our sun-soaked rights.

Late-night stories by the fire,
With glowing embers, we never tire.
In this slice of life's sweet jest,
We find ourselves, we are the best!